15th June, 1215

After King John's barons rebel against what they see as his excessive taxation and royal privileges, he is forced to sign the Magna Carta with them at Runnymede. This is the first written law to establish and limit royal rights.

1216

The barons continue to rebel against King John despite the signing of the Magna Carta, enlisting the help of the French in trying to dethrone the monarch.

October 1216

John dies and his nine-year-old son is crowned Henry III.

Map of castles across Britain

Many castles were built in Britain in the centuries following the Norman invasion in 1066 AD. A lot of the castles now only exist in ruined form. This map shows the locations of some of the most significant medieval castles built in England, Scotland and Wales.

Scotland

Glamis

Stirling

Edinburgh

Berwick-upon-Tweed

Roxburgh

Alnwick

Durham

England

Conwy

Caernarfon

Hedingham

Harlech

Shrewsbury

Wales

Orford

Ludlow

Bedford

Goodrich

Oxford

Rochester

Raglan

Queenborou

Gloucester

Windsor

Dover

Bodiam

London

Hastings

Castle-an-Dinas

Pevensey

Author:
Jacqueline Morley studied English at Oxford University. She has taught English and history and now works as a freelance writer. She has written historical fiction and nonfiction for children.

Artist:
David Antram was born in Brighton, England, in 1958. He studied at Eastbourne College of Art and then worked in advertising for fifteen years before becoming a full-time artist. He has illustrated many children's nonfiction books.

Series creator:
David Salariya was born in Dundee, Scotland. He has illustrated a wide range of books and has created and designed many new series for publishers in the UK and overseas. He established The Salariya Book Company in 1989. He lives in Brighton, England, with his wife, illustrator Shirley Willis, and their son Jonathan.

Editor: **Stephen Haynes**

Editorial Assistants: **Mark Williams, Tanya Kant**

Published in Great Britain in MMXIX by
Book House, an imprint of
The Salariya Book Company Ltd
25 Marlborough Place, Brighton BN1 1UB
www.salariya.com

ISBN: 978-1-912904-06-8

© The Salariya Book Company Ltd MMXIX

1 3 5 7 9 8 6 4 2

A CIP catalogue record for this book is available from the British Library.
Printed and bound in China.

Visit
www.salariya.com
for our online catalogue and
free fun stuff.

PAPER FROM
SUSTAINABLE FORESTS

MUCH of the villeins' own harvest goes to the lord as rent. This poor woman is paying her rent in eggs – only the rich use money.

MOST VILLEIN HOMES have just two rooms; one of them is for the animals. Your father's house is much grander – it has three rooms!

Handy hint

Five men can harvest two acres (0.8 hectare) in a day, as every bailiff knows. Don't let them take longer – they're just being lazy.

Rochester castle

Rochester cathedral

Why would they want **her** in the castle?

I suppose she thinks she's better than us.

In the bailey

It's the great day! You've come with your father to the castle. When you pass through its gate into the bailey – that's the area inside the castle walls – you're amazed to find that it's just like a busy village. There are stables, barracks and all sorts of other wooden buildings around the walls. Everything you need to live on is here. There's a small farm with vegetable plots, cow sheds, a poultry yard and a dairy. In the big central space, men-at-arms are being drilled.

WHILE YOUR father talks with the marshal (the head of military supplies), you watch the farrier shoeing a huge warhorse. 'A warhorse is the most expensive thing a knight has to buy,' he tells you.

Gatehouse

I thought this was a friendly match!

MEN-AT-ARMS (soldiers who are not knights) wrestle to keep fit while they're not on guard duty. When a lord needs warriors, he summons knights from their estates.

So... What's your excuse?

THESE VILLEINS are accused of grinding their corn at home instead of paying to have it ground at the lord's mill. They'll be tried by the sheriff at his court in the castle.

Key to the bailey

(Note: the wooden buildings have not survived – we can only guess what they were like.)

1 Barracks
2 Armoury
3 Smithy
4 Stables
5 Kennels
6 Almonry
7 Storage barn
8 Chapel and belfry
9 Guesthouse
10 Hall and buttery
11 Kitchen
12 Bakehouse
13 Brewhouse
14 Laundry
15 Dispensary
16 Chandlery
17 Poultry yard
18 Cattle shed
19 Dairy
20 Hay barn
21 Tool and wagon shed

Handy hint

A well-stocked bailey is no use if attackers can get in. Protect it with a strong gatehouse and a drawbridge over a moat.

Keep

Exercise yard

Kitchen garden

Cattle yard

Orchard

Outer wall or curtain wall

The keep

'**W**ill I be seeing the lord of the castle?' you ask nervously when you reach the keep – the castle's main tower. Your father laughs. 'No, he's much too important. He's the Lord Archbishop of Canterbury – the most important churchman in the country. He's hardly ever here. The castle is run by his deputy, the constable. He's an important baron and you'll be serving his wife.'

Archbishop's private apartments

Archbishop's private chapel

Furniture covered up

Trestle table packed away

Archbishop's state rooms

Sheriff's court in the Great Hall

Haven't I seen you here before?

Storage rooms at ground level

Your new job

YOUR FATHER leaves you with the chamberlain, a busy man in charge of household affairs. He takes you to the Great Chamber where the ladies spend the day. The constable's wife lives like a great lady, with damsels (ladies-in-waiting) to wait on her. One of the older ladies explains your duties. Clearly she doesn't think much of you. 'You need new clothes,' she says. 'We don't want ragamuffins. You'll get some as Christmas pay. Till then you'll wear hand-me-downs.'

A cutaway view of the castle keep.

If attackers ever break into the bailey, the castle dwellers can shut themselves safe and snug inside the keep. Its walls are thick, its windows small and high, and its entry well protected. Its cellars are stocked with food and weapons, and it has its own well. The first floor, where the constable lives, is split by a wall into two large rooms: the hall, where he conducts business, and the Great Chamber for family use. The Archbishop's rooms above are closed up until he comes.

Handy hint

Medieval advice to an untrained servant: 'Do not claw your back as if you were after a flea, or stroke your hair as if you sought a louse.'

And stand up straight when I'm talking to you!

She was just the same when I started working here.

I want to go home.

15

A castle day

At noon everyone eats in the hall in the bailey. The constable, his lady and the household officials sit at the 'high table' at the top end of the hall. The rest sit at trestle tables down the length of the hall, with the more important people closer to the high table. You're at the other end, next to a smug-looking page. He spoons some stew onto his trencher (the slice of bread that's used as a plate). You copy him so he'll think you know how to behave. Then he starts talking French – the language of the ruling classes – just to show off.

Bonjour.

How many robes has she got?

Cock-a-doodle-do!

IT'S MORNING. Horror! Last night you forgot to get water for the ladies' morning wash. You sneak to the indoor well in the hall while the men are still putting away their beds – strictly forbidden!

NEXT you help the ladies dress. You stoke the fire and warm their clothes in front of it. You help them pull on their stockings and hold the mirror while they do their hair.

YOU PUT the daytime cover on her ladyship's bed, tie back its curtains and put away the maids' truckle beds. Then you go to Mass, which everyone attends in the bailey chapel.

THE ELDERLY, sour-tempered damsel takes you to the wardrobe, a room where clothes are stored. Here you spend the morning cleaning fur-lined robes by rubbing them with bran.

IN THE AFTERNOON the ladies hunt with falcons. The constable's lady keeps hers in the Great Chamber. You have to sweep up its droppings and put clean rushes on the floor.

EVERY spare moment must be spent spinning wool into thread. When the ladies return, you are beaten with your distaff for letting the dog relieve itself on the rushes.

THE LADY has a bath quite often – once a month or so – in a big half-barrel that is lined with cloth in case of splinters. You have to keep refilling it with hot water.

YOU SLEEP on a straw pallet at the draughtier end of the room. From where you lie there's a strong whiff from the garderobe (toilet). It's worse than your outhouse at home.

17

From page to knight

EVERY PAGE hopes to become a squire – and every squire hopes to become a knight.

THE NIGHT before the knighting ceremony, the squire takes a bath and dresses in white to symbolise his purity of spirit.

HE SPENDS all night praying in the chapel. The next morning, he makes his confession to the priest and hears Mass.

THE PRIEST blesses the squire's sword. The lord then 'dubs' him knight by striking him on the shoulder with this same sword.

That smug page is so full of himself, you could kick him. 'My father is a baron and lives in a castle,' he tells you, 'so of course he's sent me away from home to get a good tough education. I've lived here since I was seven. I'm learning to be a knight, and when I'm fourteen they'll make me a squire like my brother. He is squire to the constable. He serves him at meals, looks after his horse and arms, and rides with him into battle. One day he'll be a knight.'

You've seen the page training in the bailey, and you think you'd make a much better squire than him. When he rode at the quintain he was much too slow and the weight swung round and hit him.

Did you ever see anything like it?

AFTER A FINAL blessing, everyone celebrates. These ceremonies are not the only way to become a knight. A lord can reward a brave man by dubbing him knight in the thick of battle.

IN PEACETIME, knights hold practice fights called mêlées. There are no rules – they just attack each other, and some get killed.

Clannng!

Thwack!

Handy hint

A squire should keep his knight's armour sparkling by rolling it in a barrel of sand, and then polishing it with a handful of horsetail plant.

Knight in shining armour? He's more like a damsel in distress!

The quintain is a swivelling target mounted on a post. It's used to practise charging with a lance.

The sandbag adds weight to the target, so you have to hit it pretty hard. Then you're supposed to get out of the way before the bag swings round.

19

The Lord comes to stay

The Lord Archbishop is on his way! Everyone is in a rush, sorting out rooms, food and stables for the huge household of officials and servants he'll be bringing with him. Great lords always travel like this. They have several homes and move from one to another. If they stayed put, their household would soon exhaust the local food supply. So they move on, taking their possessions with them. The Archbishop brings his clothes, portable furniture, magnificent hangings, bedspreads, household linen, chapel furnishings, kitchen equipment, church candles and barrels of best French wine.

Fit for a lord?

THE ARCHBISHOP'S officials arrive a few days ahead to make sure his rooms are in order. Does the chimney still smoke; do the shutters fit; are the hangings up?

That won't do!

HIS STEWARD insists that the archbishop's chamber needs whitewashing and that there must be a better chest for displaying his gold dishes when they arrive.

HIS BAKER comes to make the archbishop's favourite French bread. He's far too important to cook it himself, of course – he gives orders to the castle staff.

Handy hint

Be prepared for a big crowd at the almonry, where charity is given to the poor. When there's a banquet, beggars flock from far and wide.

IN HIS STATE CHAMBER, the Archbishop is holding a banquet for local nobles. The walls are hung with painted cloths, and a splendid canopy hangs over his throne. The high table is elegantly draped and set with gold plates. Trumpeters herald each course, and his carver kneels before him, waiting to serve. Musicians play in the gallery.

21

Rebel barons

LONDONERS are backing the rebel barons at the moment – but if John returns with a foreign army, they may be forced to change their minds.

THE CONSTABLE welcomes the barons.

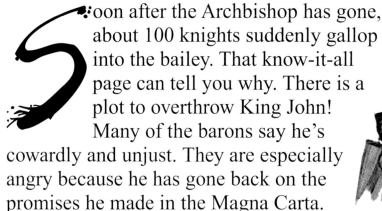

Soon after the Archbishop has gone, about 100 knights suddenly gallop into the bailey. That know-it-all page can tell you why. There is a plot to overthrow King John! Many of the barons say he's cowardly and unjust. They are especially angry because he has gone back on the promises he made in the Magna Carta.

John is at Dover on the south coast, waiting for foreign help. Rochester castle controls the route from Dover to London, so the Archbishop is letting the barons take over the castle to stop the King from returning to the capital.

Squawk!

Uh... that's it!

BUT THE CASTLE is not ready for more visitors so soon after the Archbishop's visit! And there are hardly any weapons in the armoury.

Plip!

THERE'S NOT much food or wine in the cellars, either. Entertaining the Archbishop has used up all the reserves.

THE REBELS raid the city of Rochester, forcing terrified citizens to give up their supplies at swordpoint.

The bridge

The rebels know they'll be outnumbered, but they're not going to surrender. They're sure the barons in London will send help soon. Until then they must prepare for a siege, so the constable has ordered everyone on the castle's estate to bring food at once. You've been sent home to take whatever your family can spare. Returning to the castle, you are horrified to find that the King's men are already there, in boats, setting fire to the struts of the bridge!

River Medway

What is a siege?

The idea of a siege is to surround the castle with troops so that the defenders cannot get out or bring supplies into the castle. Once they have run out of food, they will have to surrender. Destroying the bridge will make it harder to get supplies to the castle.

I hope we can get back in.

THE BOATS have been fought off, but your heart is in your mouth. Will the bridge still support the cart, the cow and you?

Creak!

SOON THE attackers are back in greater numbers. They destroy the bridge and take over the city.

24

KING JOHN uses the cathedral as a stable for his horses. The clergy are horrified.

SAFELY BACK in the castle, you see that the hill overlooking the bailey is covered with tents and armed men. Will you be safe for long?

Casualties

The siege is in its second week now. Scared and exhausted, you're in the keep, digging crossbow bolts out of men's flesh and binding their bleeding wounds. There are a thousand of the king's men outside, firing crossbows at the defenders on the outer walls and trying to put up scaling ladders.

Worse still, five mighty trebuchets are hurling rocks into the bailey, smashing its wooden buildings to bits and pounding the stone walls.

A TREBUCHET works like a seesaw. A giant boulder is placed in the sling. The sling arm is pulled down with a winch. The arm is then released – and a huge weight on the other end makes the arm shoot up again and hurl the boulder into the air.

Sling

Sling arm

Trebuchet

Winch

Weight (box of boulders)

The wall's down!

They're getting into the bailey!

A CONSTANT RAIN of boulders on one part of the wall produces first a crack, then crumbling and then collapse.

Don't worry about him, dear. At least he's still well enough to scream.

Handy hint

Spiral stairs in the keep turn clockwise. That gives you elbow-room (if you're right-handed) to swing your sword against an attacker climbing up towards you.

YOU THROW a firepot yourself, just to show that useless page, struggling with his crossbow, that you can fight too.

HE'S YANKED the bowstring into place at last! He takes aim at someone who looks very like the King. But a rebel knight reminds him that it would be a sin to kill an anointed king – even a bad one.

Unh

Pant!

Oh... yes... I suppose so.

DEFENDERS on the roof of the keep are calling for firepots (bombs made of clay pots filled with tar and lighted rags) to drop on the enemy below.

The tower collapses

It's week five of the siege. Everybody who escaped death when the bailey fell has fled to the keep. Conditions here are dreadful. People are crowded together, with barely any room to lie down to sleep. Very soon the food will run out. The trebuchets are still pounding, though surely they can't make much of a dent in the walls of the keep – these walls are nearly 4 metres thick. The enemy's ladders are useless too: the keep is much too high for them to scale. Perhaps you can hold out until help arrives from London – or perhaps not...

Uh-oh!

ONE DAY, while dressing wounds in the south tower of the keep, you notice that the surface of the water in a storage jar is quivering. What could be making the tower vibrate? You decide to raise the alarm.

THE TOWER is being mined! The king's men are digging a tunnel underneath the base of the tower. The tunnel's timber roof is held up by wooden supports, or props.

Arrow slit

Baskets of earth

Wooden shelter covered with animal hides

Pit props

Talus (stone ramp to protect base of wall)

THE MINERS carry props in and take earth out under a protective shelter.

Mine

28

THE MINERS make a deep cavity under the tower and pack it with brushwood.

King John has sent for 40 pigs.

Oink!

NEXT, they put pig fat on the brushwood and light it. That sets the props on fire. When they burn through, the ceiling collapses. Then the ground gives way, and the tower falls.

Handy hint

Miners beware! Defenders will try to drop firepots on your shelter. Cover it with hides and keep them wet.

RUMBLE!

CRASH!

This way, lads! We've got them cornered now!

Holding out in the keep

A quarter of the keep has crashed to the ground. The king's men have poured into the Great Chamber, but they cannot get control of the whole keep. The rebels have barred the connecting doors between the Chamber and the Hall and are fighting from there. They have almost no food left and nothing to drink but water – a liquid considered too dirty to drink and usually used only for washing. You are simmering a few scraps of horsemeat when you see the door leading to the floor above begin to open. John's men are trying to get in from upstairs! The guard is too quick for them this time, but how much longer can the rebels hold out?

If you can't fight, you can't eat!

...that's what I heard!

How awful!

THERE'S NOT enough food to go around, so the rebels force everyone who cannot fight to leave – even though they are bound to be captured by the enemy.

YOU DON'T WANT to be flung to the enemy so you hide as best you can. By the time you're noticed, no one has time to bother with you.

YOU HEAR what happened to the ones who did go: King John had their hands and feet cut off!

Goodbye to the castle

KING JOHN is thinking of celebrating his victory by having every one of the rebels hanged.

> Nobody messes with me!

Starvation finally forces the rebels to surrender, after nearly two months of bitter siege. By this time you hardly care what happens; the enemy will kill you if the hunger doesn't. Luckily you are far too lowly for anyone to bother with you. Even the rebels are spared by the King's greed and cowardice. He's afraid that if he punishes the barons now, they'll get even later. He seizes the castle and staffs it with people loyal to himself.

> I have a cunning plan...

BUT A FOREIGN captain has a better idea: the King should give each of his pals a rebel to hold for ransom (keeping the most valuable for himself, of course).

THE KING still wants a bit of fun, so he hangs just one crossbowman, on grounds of ingratitude: the man had been raised in the royal household, so he should have been loyal.

> Don't you worry about them, my girl - serves those rebels right!

> Pig fat! They used pig fat!

Now your father is no longer bailiff, and you're back home working on the land. You feel sorry for that wretched line of rebels being led off to rot in castle prisons for who knows how long. What a joy to know you don't ever have to set foot in a castle again!

Burp!

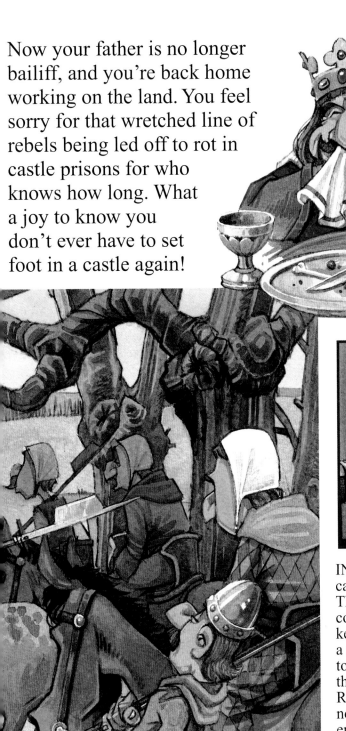

Handy hint

Don't let an important captive go too cheaply. The longer you hold on to him, the more his family may be willing to fork over for him.

What came next?

WAR BETWEEN the King and the barons continued. But in 1216, John fell ill and died after overeating at a dinner given in his honor.

JOHN'S NINE-YEAR-OLD SON became King Henry III. He wisely made peace with the barons by giving back most of the rights that John had taken from them.

IN 1227 Rochester castle was repaired. The collapsed corner of the keep was given a modern round tower in place of the old square one. Round towers have no corners for the enemy to hide behind.

Glossary* *(Some other important words are explained in the text.)

Almonry The office where charity was given to the poor.

Anointed king A king who has been crowned in a ceremony which includes a blessing with sacred oil.

Armoury A store for armour and weapons.

Bailiff The official in charge of farming on a lord's estate.

Barracks Soldiers' living quarters.

Bolt A short, thick arrow shot from a crossbow.

Brewhouse A place where ale was brewed from malted grain. Ale was safer to drink than untreated water.

Buttery The place where wine and beer were kept, in 'butts' (barrels).

Chamberlain The official in charge of a lord's household arrangements.

Chandlery A place where candles were made.

Constable The commander of a castle.

Damsel A young lady, or a lady-in-waiting.

Dispensary A place where medicines were made.

Distaff A tool for spinning wool to make thread.

Estate The land belonging to a castle.

Farrier An officer who looked after horses.

Great Chamber The second most important room in the keep. It was a more private living space for the lord and his family.

Hall The main room of a keep. Used for official business such as trying criminals and receiving visitors, it was also a communal dining room and sleeping quarters.

Knight A mounted warrior who fought for his lord and was given an estate in return.

Magna Carta A famous legal agreement made in June 1215 between King John and his barons. It removed some power from the king and gave certain rights to the people.

Man-at-arms A highly trained soldier without the status of a knight.

Marshal The official in charge of stabling, hunting and military forces.

Mêlée A fighting contest between groups of knights. A winner kept his opponent's horse – a valuable prize.

Moat A defensive ditch, usually filled with water.

Page A boy of knightly family sent from home to train for knighthood.

Pallet A thin mattress stuffed with straw.

Ransom Money paid for the release of a prisoner. Holding important prisoners for ransom was a normal part of medieval warfare.

Reeve An official elected annually by estate workers to represent their interests with the bailiff and the courts.

Rushes Marsh plants whose long, stiff, grasslike leaves were used as disposable floor coverings.

Scaling ladder A long ladder used by attackers to climb a wall.

Sheriff An officer who enforced the law in a county.

Smithy A blacksmith's workshop.

Squire A youth in the second stage of knightly training who acts as a servant to a knight.

Trencher A slice of stale bread used as a plate, or a wooden plate.

Truckle bed A low bed on wheels, used by a servant. It was put away beneath the master's or mistress's bed.

Villein A peasant entirely under the control of his lord, not owning the land he lived on and not allowed to leave it.

Index

Richard the Lionheart

Richard I became known as Richard the Lionheart because of his brave adventures in the Middle East during the Third Crusade to take back control of Jerusalem for the Christians from Saladin, its Muslim ruler. He was a popular figure in his own time and is still depicted in legend as a good and kind ruler to this day.

However, many modern historians have a more critical opinion of him. We know that he spent huge amounts of money on equipment and men for his trips abroad and had a fairly careless attitude towards the care of the country over which he reigned. He spent far more time out of England than he did within it during his time as king. He could also be quick to anger and cruel with those who resisted his demands.

Legend of Robin Hood

King John's ruthless oppression of the rebellious barons and his brother's absence from England during his crusades in the Middle East contributed to the famous legend of Robin Hood and his gang of merry men. It is not known whether a real-life Robin Hood ever existed and served as inspiration for the character, but over the centuries the basic outline of the story has become fairly well-established and familiar to audiences around the world. This story depicts Robin Hood as a noble outlaw who robs from the rich to give to the poor in defiance of the greedy rule of King John and his assistant, the Sheriff of Nottingham. John is usually depicted as having usurped his kind-hearted brother Richard's throne during his time away from England. The story has been retold many times up to the present day in literature, television and film productions.

Castle prison facts

Enemies who were caught during battle might be imprisoned in a castle. In castles, prison cells were often built above the main gates in the outer walls. This stopped dangerous prisoners from getting too close to the castle keep or the central tower of the castle. Other castle prisons were hidden deep below ground or in high towers. Sometimes cells were just metal cages hung outside the castle.

Little ease

This was a tiny room hollowed out of a castle wall. Some of these cramped chambers were so small that prisoners could not lie down, sit comfortably, or even turn around.

Noble prisoners

Some castles had private rooms where rich or noble prisoners were locked up in nice surroundings. They might even be allowed to stroll in the castle's gardens.

Oubliette

An oubliette was a narrow, tube-shaped prison, without windows. The only way in was through a trapdoor at the top. Prisoners were lowered down on a rope and left to rot. Sometimes water seeped in from the bottom and they drowned.

Towers

Tall stone towers kept prisoners high in the air. They were designed to prevent escapes and hide prisoners away from friends who might help them.